Judith Beveridge | Devadatta's Poems

New Poems

GIRAMONDO POETS

Judith Beveridge | Devadatta's Poems

First published 2014
from the Writing & Society Research Centre
at the University of Western Sydney
by the Giramondo Publishing Company
PO Box 752 Artarmon NSW 1570 Australia
www.giramondopublishing.com

Designed by Harry Williamson
Typeset by Andrew Davies
in 9.5/16.5 pt Baskerville

Printed and bound by Ligare
Distributed in Australia by NewSouth Books

National Library of Australia
Cataloguing-in-Publication data:

Beveridge, Judith –
Devadatta's Poems / Judith Beveridge
ISBN 9781922146526
(pbk)

A821.3

For Eileen Chong and Robert Joannides

Also by Judith Beveridge

The Domesticity of Giraffes
Accidental Grace
Wolf Notes
Storm and Honey
Hook and Eye: a selection of poems (USA)
Peregrine (chapbook)
How to Love Bats (chapbook)

Acknowledgements

Grateful acknowledgement is made to the editors of the following anthologies and journals in which many of these poems first appeared: *Australian Book Review, Australian Weekend Review, Axon, HEAT, Island, Mascara, Southerly, The Australian Book of Love Poetry 2013, The Best Australian Poems 2010, The Best Australian Poems 2013, The Warwick Review* (UK).

I would like to thank the Literature Board of the Australia Council for the New Work Grant which was of enormous assistance in the writing of this book.

Special thanks to Adrian Wiggins for the gift of a new *Roget's International Thesaurus, Seventh Edition*, which has provided me with much inspiration and linguistic fuel.

For advice on the manuscript my sincere thanks to Stephen Edgar and for advice on individual poems my thanks to the Sunday Poetry group. I am indebted to Dr Mark Allon for providing me with historical advice.

Thanks also to Ivor Indyk and Alice Grundy.

Contents

Words are birds perceived
in a secret forest
fed by nerve and vein they hop
from twig to twig and up
an ivory ladder to the top
where it is light and they remain
and are believed

MAY SWENSON, 'The Process'

Introduction

All poems in the sequence are written in the voice of Devadatta. According to Pāli datung, Devadatta lived in the sixth century BCE in India. He was a cousin of Siddhattha Gotama, the Buddha. Both Devadatta and Siddhattha were *khattiyas* (Sanskrit: *Kshatriya*), members of the warrior or ministerial caste, which at the time was the most prominent caste in northern India. Devadatta came from the town of Kapilavatthu, the capital of the northern state of Sakiya. The remains of the city are today situated on the Indian-Nepalese border at the town of Tilaurakot.

The Sakiyas were a republic, but according to tradition, they were ruled by Suddhodana, Devadatta's uncle and the father of Siddhattha.

Sakiya was a vassal-state to neighbouring Kosala, a powerful kingdom to the west that controlled most of the eastern part of what is today Uttar Pradesh. Sakiya was in a relatively weak position and inevitably destined to be annexed by one of the great powers that surrounded it on all sides. In fact, Kapilavatthu was destroyed by the ruler of Kosala, Vidudabha, in approximately 485 BCE shortly before the Buddha died. He put to death all its citizens of military age and then set fire to the town.

In approximately 536 BCE, Siddhattha left Kapilavatthu and embarked on a mendicant life around central India in search of enlightenment. Devadatta remained in Kapilavatthu. At the age of 35, the Buddha preached his first Discourse in Sarnath, a town a little to the north of Benares. Here he founded the Order (Sangha) of monks, which Devadatta joined in approximately 527 BCE.

Later, Devadatta tried in various ways to usurp control of the Order, including causing a schism and attempting to murder the Buddha on three occasions, all of which were unsuccessful. During this time, Devadatta developed a friendship with Prince Ajatasattu, the son of King Bimbisara of Magadha, who had converted to Buddhism. Both men had ambitions of leadership: Devadatta of the Sangha and Ajatasattu of the Kingdom of Magadha.

Devadatta's Poems imaginatively traces Devadatta's

time as a monk in Sarnath and later in Rajagaha during his time of plotting. I have telescoped down much of the time frame, and while I have followed the basic narrative found in the Pāli Canon, I have used a great deal of poetic licence, inventing characters and scenarios, and at times being deliberately historically inaccurate. I have interpreted the character of Devadatta through my own lens. This sequence has been *highly* fictionalised and dramatised.

Some commentators say that Devadatta was the brother of Yasodhara, Siddhattha's wife, but I have also read that Devadatta was a suitor to Yasodhara, but he failed to win her hand in a test of arms, and that part of Devadatta's animosity towards the Buddha was based on jealousy. This is the tack I have taken in the sequence. I have also deviated from the historical narrative by making Devadatta much more lascivious and pleasure seeking, but also more wistful and equivocal than is suggested in the Pāli Canon. The Pāli Canon is the standard collection of scriptures in the Theravada Buddhist tradition, as preserved in the Pāli language. It is the most complete early Buddhist canon and was composed in north India, and preserved orally until it was written down during the Fourth Buddhist Council in Sri Lanka in 29 BCE, approximately 454 years after the death of Buddha.

Getting to Sarnath

To get to the monastery outside Sarnath
I had to cross the Ghagara and Gomati rivers.
I had to take a mule
over the Churian foothills where there were bands
of marauding, blue-skinned hunters.
I had to pass into the jungles

full of tigers, rhinoceros, wild dogs. I had to cross
the fields and the towns owned by the Koliya
and Moriya clans
who hate all Sakiyans and with whom we are
in bitter dispute over pasture and irrigation rights.
All the time I pictured

Siddhattha sitting among the deer and his soft-soled monks.
Siddhattha who betrayed his caste, his kingdom
and wandered off
like a homeless ox herd. I'd spent years taking up
my profession of arms, overseeing the cultivation
of the fields, helping

his father with disputes, the tedious collections
of levies and spring harvest taxes.
Now I'm sitting
in a vine-covered hut in heat-shimmering air.
I should gather stones off a turning and make
a memorial to all the years

I took my measure among bullock droppings,
    the white bones in the fields, to all the years
        I felt as grey
and as ghostly as chaff. I should make a shrine
    to my new-fangled life, to Siddhattha, and his odd
        horde of riffraff.

Little

I know I'd better get used to living on little –
dappled shadows, handfuls of rice, narrow footpaths,
a view of the sky through a slat. Siddhattha is just
a streak, a strip of willow bark, a robe and loincloth
his only bulk. Now, over the plain there's a slip

of moon like a dew-starched wing declaring itself
against the heat. Haze in the distance and a thread of smoke.
A scarlet ibis flies across the evening. Where
it joins the flock, the river bank seems to be flaming,
burning like a ghat. The sun strikes an outcrop

of basalt and near the creek I see some frogs
lying across lily pads and gleaming like bright
splatters of butterfat. Soon night will fall over
the shoulders of the foothills and across the plains
dark as the pelt of a black doe. I'll make

an undergarment from the soft inner bark of some
banyans and secure it with a strong girdle of grass,
then I'll warm my hands over a fire of cowpats.
Come morning, I might wake to the sounds of parrots,
or to ox carts clattering over some holes and ruts.

Ground Swell

So many insects clicking, jumping up against my legs
with the torsional stress of little springs.
So many mouths dressing the flax,
the scutch, quitch and barley, wheat and sesame;
so many mouths
in a chirl and chirm.
I can hear them all in a tidal race
over sweet flag and gale, sorghum and sorrel;
insects eating away petals
and grain heads,
hanging on in a swirl of wind, hanging on
as the tails of mules
come at them
like the swippling swishes of fly-maddened flails.
They scritch from the briar tangles,
from leaves and twigs; all around I hear the scrape
of their winnowing legs.
So many insects
loose in the wind, loose in the grasses,
loose in the mustard, loose in the thistles and furze;
a wing-storm crackling,
poised, then shifting – a blur, a flurry –
over witch hazel,
hyssop, trillium and mallow.
So many insects chipping for food, pricking their songs
over my arms and head.

Alms Round, Sarnath

I smell ripe figs, dates, pomegranates; cumin and onions
sizzling in hot ghee. There are piles of sesame and honey cakes,
teas scented with cinnamon and cloves, but we must wait

along the town's outskirts, keep our eyes downcast,
try to be grateful for whatever's given. Mostly all I'm given
are scrawny parings of stalks, maggoty wheat crawling

in the centre of my hands. Don't these other monks
want to look these folk squarely in the eyes and demand
mangos, melons and handpicked beans? Don't they want

to stuff their mouths full of rice and roasted coconut,
with almonds, cashews and pickled beets? Aren't they tired
of seeing their bowls as bare as their shaved heads?

I want to tell Buddha to chew his rules about patience
and frugality into a sloppy cud. I want to hold my bowl out
as boldly as a symbol and clang it loudly with my spoon.

I want to tell these miserable, skinflint, pinch-fisted folk
to stop tossing us husks, rinds, cores, thorns, rats' tails,
roosters' claws and – oh! – so many stinking lepers' thumbs!

Wanting Yasodhara

I wanted to be the one to lift the sari
    from her nakedness, to smell her scent of myrrh,
        to offer her the dissolute bewitchment
of the tamarack wine. I wanted to be
    the one to paint her palms and feet with camphire,

        to hear the lissom sibilance
of her bracelets when they slipped up and down
    her arms, to see her dance and swirl
        her scarves about her head in dizzying
vapours, to give her jewels of pink corundum,

    to touch her hair, fine-grained as polished ebony.
        When the Brahmins lit the altars,
cut the throats of ten strong oxen, then poured
    perfumed ghee over hers and my cousin's garlanded arms,
        I wanted to scour Siddhattha's heart

from his body with my hands. And though it's been years
    since the wedding, and though I'm far
        from Kapilavatthu now, I still want
to unwrap her sari from her body and lift her hair
    from her shoulders with my sorrow-worn hands.

Riders

When we were youths, we'd mount our horses and ride.
I'd be careless, a daredevil. He'd be cautious,
always solicitous of the horse. At the Spring Festivals
I could always keep my mount, stay on a bucking

stallion's back through any terrain: mud, stones,
slipping scree. Usually, they'd find Siddhattha thrown off,
dazed, wandering through the wheat and mustard fields.
I'd circle him, laugh at him, tell him his horse belonged

on a wooden carousel…Ah, it's time for me to take
the reins again, turn this solemn place into a carnival,
a place with new rules – the Sangha in full carousal –
and Siddhattha, once more, slipped from the saddle.

To Ananda

Ananda, do you remember our walks along
the shores of Raghaya pond? We'd watch the water

turn pellucid lilac in the light of the late summer sun.
Over the stones the runnels tinkled like dancers

with bells at their toes; chipping sparrows twittered
like fine shiftings of marl. Do you remember

the herons stepping over the sand, regally bearing
themselves as if they held public office, and the egrets,

white robed as tax collectors with a determination
for profit, how they'd stab unendingly at the reeds?

We'd stroll, kneel at the shore, find stones and shells
to barter, then feed handfuls of banana and papaya

to our snaggle-toothed camel. Brother, do you remember
that man we'd laugh at, the old wanderer with hair

like a matted root ball, with eyelids like the carapaces
of dead dung beetles; the one we'd see drinking

from a ditch, bending down beside a sow, a goat
and a pariah dog; the one who looked as if he'd spent

too long roaming sun-baked plains, too long sucking
on leaves of the mind-enfeebling monkey-pod tree?

Well, look at me now, Ananda, and you might think
I'm that man. I'm leaning into the cheap shade

of a sassafras. I've been three months in this monastery,
barely anything to eat but wisps of smoke. But I'm

still plotting my backyard empires; and even in this
heat, expecting fine glassy water to tickle my feet.

Flower Stall

Whenever I come to Sarnath,
I hope I can beg in the artisans' quarters so I can watch
the garland makers' daughters. Now, I watch them
cup their fingers round the flowers, twist the stems
and draw the threads up with long bare sweeps

of their arms. I dream
they harvest me, nectar me, flavour me with the pollen-scented
fingers they wipe across their hair, down their bodices,
over their breasts. I dream their mouths festoon mine.

In Sarnath, no matter
what stern monk is with me on my rounds, no matter
what precepts or verses I'll recite, I know I'll never
stop wishing my face and robes can be stained not with mud,
or common potter's clay; not with spills of gruel,

or curd, or ghee;
not with fruit, or grease, or drips of whey; not with daubs
of honey, or splotches of spice, but with the smears and smutches
from each garland maker's daughter's fecund fingers.

Monastery: Poverty and Slim Pickings

We have no balms, no ointments, no tinctures.
We have no bandages of muslin or linen – our only dressings
are lichen, hair-grass and mud, our poultices are sods.
Our only stitches are the pincers and jaws of long
red ants cinching shut our wounds when their bodies

are severed from their heads. Does Siddhattha
think our hands aren't polluted, that our sores aren't infected,
that our bums are always clean, that our teeth
have no caries? With the monsoon and poor alms,
one by one we fall ill – and our only medicine

is putrefied cattle urine. We have no syrups,
no elixirs, no drugs – so we'd better not get abscesses
on our gums, ulcers on our shins, no more boils on our buttocks –
though all of us have itches, diseases of the skin
because we dress in tatters: rags that we pull from dust

heaps and charnel fields. If we want sunshades
we use our hands; if we need mosquito fans we use fronds;
our walking staffs are branches felled by the wind. And –
it wouldn't surprise me to learn – our water pots are cinerary urns,
and our alms bowls the skulls of disinterred dogs.

At Rajkote, after the Rains Retreat

I had just walked out of the reeds at the confluence
of two rivers. Brown frogs stuck in my hair like gouts
of flung mud, my skin was whip-stitched, lacerated
with leeches. I was walking a path hazardous
with snakes, meridians breaching my footsteps

while I mush-stepped in the high grass. I cried out
like someone who'd bled on the wrong altars. Half-naked,
I blew into town like unsorted litter. The people
wanted to slit my throat, so I wandered away to one
of the abandoned huts by the river. Gibbons and rats

stole my fruit. My feet were sore, split like seeds.
My head wobbled in the heat like a dog's, then I queered
my nostrils at an angle to the ghats. I could reckon
a hare's smell down to a point, accurate as a compass.
I could hear geese hiss, swaying their necks.

At dusk I listened to the rain gentle the surface
of the river. Little by little it put my mind right.
Finally, my thoughts came as airily as insects skimming
over a pond; a peace came over me that had the equanimity
of snow. Suddenly, I knew I could move on.

Her Hair

At night I think of her hair like a free hoard
of honey in my hands. Sometimes I imagine she is letting
me thread jasmine, or strips of perfumed bark through her hair;
that I'm rolling her hair into a thick bun at her nape,
dressing it with oil, or adorning it with feathers.

Sometimes I dream she lets me colour her parting
with the same vermillion stick she'll later apply to her lips.
I think of her hair and I smell leaf musk, myrrh,
then the peregrine rain. When insects fizz and snap
at the lamplight, I dream they are the sound of the teeth

of one of her ivory combs, breaking as I draw them
down those heavy strands, the light stroking,
then filling her hair with shadow. When the days
and nights pass with unremitting rain, I dream I hear the sighs
of her bracelets slipping into my secret whisperings

of her name. But some nights, all I can hear is her
cracking in half all of her gem-studded combs; then the rasp
and harrow of the stone-handled knife: Yasodhara
hacking her hair back to her scalp – the *flump* of it falling –
and Yasodhara sobbing out Siddhattha's name.

Back in the Monastery, Sarnath

In the waxing and waning fortnights of the moon
I will pray to the light and dark goddesses. I will pray
to Elephant-Face, Lion-Face, Bloody-Eyes and Lolling-Tongue.
I will invoke the Mother of the Three Worlds,
the goddess who bears no weapon, but who carries
a cooking pot and a spoon. I will call upon the Slayer

of the Bull Demon, The Woman of Beautiful
Wild Hair, Daughter of the Mountain whose shrines
are tamarisk and tangled rabbit berry. I will worship
the goddess who sits at the threshold of time, stern
doorkeeper with her cattle goad, her noose, and her hatchet.
I will worship The Cool Goddess even when floods

are high and I have to wade through deep water
to reach her temple, which is gloomy and dark but for
the butter lamps on her altar. Buddha says the universe
is not the work of a creator. He says it appears, is dissolved
of its own accord; that gods and goddesses may exist,
but what prevails is karma. But I think I'll always

summon the two sisters, Lion-Face and Bloody-Eyes,
when I pass a certain village, a certain crossroad;
that I'll always see the silver face of the Cool Goddess
in the knothole of a fragrant cedar; that I'll always
think of the moon as a stone from a ruined temple
that must be worshipped, no matter how it lies.

Tailspin

I sit and muse on Yasodhara,
I smell her hair, her scent of jasmine. I want
to hear the Buddha's doctrines. I want to say my prayers
and mantras, but I smell her hair, her scent of jasmine. I sway
about like a flute-charmed cobra. I want to say my prayers
and mantras, but my head aches, my legs and my
back again. I find it hard to have

self-discipline, my head aches,
my legs, then my back again. I try to ponder karma,
dukkha, the turning of the wheel of law, but I find it hard
to gain self-discipline. I smell her hair, her scent of jasmine, my
mind can't shift its tuneless timbre, my head aches, my legs,
then my back again. I want to hear the Buddha's
doctrines, to ponder karma,

dukkha, the turning of the wheel
of law. I want to say my prayers and mantras,
but I sit and muse on Yasodhara. I smell her hair,
her scent of jasmine. I sway about like a flute-charmed cobra,
my mind can't shift its tuneless timbre, I want
to hear the Buddha's doctrines, but I sit and muse
on Yasodhara, I smell her hair.

The Past

Hard to believe I loved Siddhattha once; now I stare
at him with a gaze as heated as an arrow in a pan
of burning coals. But I remember how we'd swing
our saddlebags over our shoulders

and scamper out of the city gates with linked arms;
how we'd stroll the path to where our ponies waited
under the apple boughs; how we'd find the grove
where the ice spring burbled

and hide in Boar's Cave and listen to squirrels
eating their hoards of whortleberries, then we'd run out,
brawling under the laurels. Sometimes when I hear
children playing with trinkets

and gimcrack, when I hear jackasses bray
as they lift their faces to the wind to smell the sheaves
of freshly cut sorghum, aromatic herbs, sassafras,
I long for our boyhoods,

the time when we made up tales about a place
we called the Forest of Bliss – where sparrows nestled
against cats, where cats slept peacefully in the feathers
of peacocks, where otters

left the fish alone, where hawks paid
no attention to the quail, where jackals lay down in the grass
with the spotted antelopes. Hard to believe we were
ever such youths, boys

with such affection and no losses yet to mourn.
Hard to believe we hardly quarrelled, that many years
passed before we stood facing one another, dressed
in horsehair plumes,

buckling swords to our tunics, ready to fight
for Yasodhara's hand. Now, I wonder when Siddhattha
shuts his eyes, does he remember the clop
of our ponies' hooves

along the sheep tracks, the sky over Kapilavatthu
when it seemed to be raked clear by a plough? Does the beauty
and bounty of Yasodhara's hair ever bedevil him
like a vulture's dark wings?

The Comb

Perhaps one day I'll throw away my bag
of carved nuts and gilded shells and never again
beseech the temptress goddesses or the presiding deities
of the gambling house. Perhaps never again

will I long for the rattle of nuts and shells
across a table or floor, for their clicking weight against
my hip as I tote them round town looking to win
what I've always wanted to win: not cows,

horses, gold; not jewels, perfumes or parasols,
but a hundred-toothed pearl and deer-horn comb.
Then perhaps I'll return home and I'll see
what I've always wanted to see, hear

what I've always wanted to hear: Yasodhara
running her thumb down all its length,
feeling the softness of its sarcenet, drawstring sheath,
then weeping for joy when she tallies the teeth.

The Test

How did Siddhattha win Yasodhara's hand
in a rival test of arms? Instead of practising archery,
chariot racing, or fencing,
Siddhattha would wander round town watching
potters mould clay and goldsmiths
purify gold. He'd help

basket-makers gather reeds from the river; help
widows, cripples, old temple dancers and mothers
of prostitutes spin
and cut cloth. The day of the contest he spent
the morning consoling an ailing couple
who'd carried

three infant sons to a burial ground.
He fashioned a flute and blew strange melodies
into the wind, then placed
around their shoulders a finely woven shawl.
But what changed when he stepped into the ring?
Was I the only one

who saw how he immediately struck a warrior pose,
how his body grew rigid as an iron pikestaff, how his gaze
shone like a blade
in a pan of sizzling coal? What shifted the odds?
We all thought he'd have trouble sheathing
his arrows, buckling

his sword. Was I the only one who saw her smile,
who saw her quick exhortative nod? Oh, little could Yasodhara
know how much
that signal would cost – and as Siddhattha let those winning
shafts and lances fly – little could he foresee
what would, one day, be lost.

My Name

I've tried mantras and prayers. I've fasted for many days
hoping I'll taste the spittle and the gall-drenched juices
known to a hungry man. I've tried pastes of ashes, cloves
and nettles. I've swallowed vinegar rinses. I've chewed

on the sourest, most bitter leaves I can find. I've even
sipped on the festering dregs lying in troughs and ditches
used by pariah dogs. Sometimes, I think only rags
from the charnel field might do it, might sop it up,

might cleanse my palate, keep the space between my
tongue and the roof of my mouth clean of the piquancy,
the round flooding softness, the sweet mango fullness,
the gushing, mouth-watering ripeness of my own name.

The Buddha at Uruvela

Look at the Buddha speaking to the crowd.
Why don't they turn away jeering, resentful? They're all
so poor. Can't they see Buddha speaks from the privilege
of a high-borne, well-heeled past? There's Sati,

the fisherman, Tissa, the doorkeeper, Dhaniya
the potter, Arittha the vulture-trainer, Citta the mahout.
And look at Sunita, the street-sweeper, smiling
as if the Buddha has offered him a life above

the scorn of insects, a life of refinements
other than dust. Look how Suppaya, the corpse bearer,
beams, as if from now on he'll make compassion
the stretcher for any – light or heavy – dispersal

of death. There are fuel-gatherers, dung-brick makers,
grass-cutters; those who've come from dust-heaps,
charnel grounds, river-sides, quarries; those
with wounds, cankers, crooked limbs. Don't these

folk know what shackles them to suffering
is not desire, as the Buddha exposits, but the hard-set,
iron-fisted system of caste. Oh why, like me, aren't
they all sick of his hubris, sick of his bombast?

Bimbisara, King of Magadha

Lately the King's conversion is on everyone's lips:
O Bimbisara's encounter with the numinous
has filled him with bliss! There's talk he'll donate
his pleasure park, Veluvana, a grove of almond
and sala trees outside the north gate of Rajagaha,

to the Sangha. Bimbisara is a kind, sagacious king,
but his son, Ajatasattu, is ambitious, has no time
for Buddha. O, I think we'll get on famously!
Already I can see the two of us lazing on a gilded
couch, filling our heads with plans, drinking cups

of koumis and playing dice. Everyone knows
Magadha is on the rise: it has iron, copper, elephants,
plentiful supplies of forest timber, the largest
army on the Gangetic Plain. Ajatasattu, one day
the Buddha's Sangha will be mine, one day

your Father's kingdom will be yours. Already
I can hear the conches blowing. I can hear the bells
of your warrior elephants as you parade through town.
I can smell the blood of the oxen sacrificed to you.
I can hear them screaming as their throats are slit.

In Rajagaha

Sariputta and Moggallana are talking on the Four
Noble Truths. Men and women come out from the market
and bazaars. In the square, someone plays a veena,
someone else a sitar. The monks will talk well
into the night. I watch the sky grow cinnabar,

in the distance I listen for the call of the nightjar,
but I only hear the turkey buzzards and the koels.
From the crowd, a woman sings, her voice
is sweet as nougat. Sariputta and Moggallana
speak about the Eightfold Path, the woman is singing

of love, deceit, misery and desire; in the square
someone plays a veena, someone else a sitar.
Finally the buzzards fly off to the sycamores;
the koels are still fluting. In the street, a woman
closes the windows and cedar shutters of her house.

Buddha's word is spreading now through Rajagaha.
But I grow sorrowful and I grow glum, wondering
if I'll ever inspire anything but windy dissonance,
if I'll ever bring to pass my coup d'etat? In the square
someone plays a veena and someone else a sitar.

Vultures Peak

Whenever I come here I don't pay much attention
to the lammergeier circling from the peaks overhead,
but I keep an eye out for falling tortoises, elephants' ribs,
jackals' jawbones. I stay on the level where the farm
women scythe and rick, scythe and rick, or pick

tithes of yellow samphire near the ponds. I don't
climb to the summit to take in the view of the valley
and the fertile plains; or, as the Buddha suggests,
spend time alone in one of the small damp caves
meditating on suffering and its causes in desire.

I stay at the base near the talus inhaling the heady
perfume of the lavender and vetch. I watch the farm
women drink and rest near the ponds, then bend
and sweat again in the sinking madder sun. I let desire
have its ground. I take my chances under falling bones.

The Toad

Suddenly I saw it in the thistle grass ballooning up
large as a puffball ready to explode. Then it belched,
put out a stink like one of Kapilavatthu's old cracked cisterns.
Now it sits in my hut like a clump of mud studded

with fine stones. Sometimes when I tire of it croaking,
I threaten to give it to the swineherd's boys to boil,
or to lob over the trees the way they do geckos and frogs.
But mostly I talk to it, splash it with pond water,

feed it slugs as thick as my thumb. Sometimes I palp
the venom glands behind its eyes and along the top
of its head with a wide ferny leaf. I don't know why
I keep it with me. Perhaps I like its long sticky tongue,

the warts on its sorrowing skin, how its stink reminds
me of home. Perhaps it gives me a model of how to sit
squat, absorbed and croak out one mantra after another.
Perhaps I just want a little fat Buddha for my own.

Watching the Moon

Moon, I've always had a fondness for you.
Perhaps because you arrive in your own halo
like a god. Perhaps because of the way
you hoard your light down to the last quarter;
how like a money-lender you hide your profit
in your smile; and how – like me – moon,
you are fated to always give way to the dark.

The Blind Soothsayer

He tells me a woman, more exquisite, more exotic than any
of the luminous objects found in the zodiac, will come into my life.
Yasodhara, I ask? He stays silent, turns to a farmer and tells him
he'll lose two sons to floodwater, a granddaughter to thieves,

his cousin and prize geese to a disease-ridden jackal. He tells
a young boy his mother will be bitten by a cobra at dawn.
Look, I don't believe in the fatal necessity of the stars, I don't
believe the lines on a hand lead to truth, but I'm tempted

to offer him more money if he'll cast his eyes further to see
what hangs at the hub of my sidereal wheel as it mills across
time and space. Now I hear him tell a woman her son will fall
madly in love with a club-footed swineherd, that her moon

in Virgo will soon turn balsamic...Ah, what a gouger he is,
a hyena, a swindler, a snake in the grass! All morning in front
of the temple, rolling his blanched eyes back into his head,
costing people's lot, pinpointing ill-luck...I could do that!

Rules

I know I shouldn't make a noise chewing food
or pick my teeth with my fingers, or scratch my head
and let my dandruff fall into my neighbour's bowl.
When the conch sounds for foot-washing, I shouldn't
fight to snatch the foot bucket. As I walk, stand,

or sit, I should recite in a calm manner: *Wonderful*
indeed is the ambrosia of liberation, the flower
of the sorrowless field of merit, the perfume
of doctrine which I shall keep always on my breath.
During the cold I should not make a bad smell

by toasting my sandals; I should not spit or throw
balls of grease into the fire. At meditation time,
I should learn to draw my robe around myself
without fanning up a breeze and causing a monk's
thoughts to stir. If truth be known, these things I can

do easily – but what I'll never do, is stop planning
how to run Buddha out of his tidy squat, how to get
the townsfolk and monks to curse him from his top-knot
down. Ah, I can almost smell it in the air now –
that scent when something sweet moulders and rots.

Conversation with Ajatasattu

At nights when I'm sleepless, I like to imagine talking
with Ajatasattu at the Palace. We're eating sweetmeats,
drinking goblets of wine when I say: *Friend, it's not uncommon,*
because of wild ambition, for folk who are consanguine
to strangle, knife, behead, or poison one another. So Ajatasattu,
put Bimbisara in a dungeon; in dung, in filth, in darkness,
no luxuries, no food, use starvation as a weapon, make him
carrion for vermin, let's have the old goat shrunken,

broken in his chains. I see Ajatasattu broadly smile,
and he summons his servant to bring more figs, more honey cakes.
I continue: *You know I think about it often, how to finish*
off my cousin. Should I use an old rogue elephant, one totally
deranged, one whose tusks could bludgeon out his brains?
Or when he's on his walk, descending Vultures Peak,
should I roll a boulder down a cliff? Our talk goes on past
midnight, and suddenly the Prince offers me some advice:

Why don't you bribe a ruffian to serve as the assassin,
then hire another villain to put that man in his coffin,
and so on down the chain? We both laugh and toast our treachery.
Then I go to sleep, feeling most relieved, as if I really
did eat a platter of figs and sweetmeats, as if I really did hear
Ajatasattu proclaim: *Devadatta, by the time of the waning*
moon, I'll have the Kingdom, you'll have the Sangha.

New Day

I walk into town with my alms bowl. The wind
seems to chant: *food, fodder, fibre, flowers, fuel.*
As I walk, there's the tang of caraway, the grassy
scent of sorrel, the subtle sweetness of thyme.

I'm not sure today why I feel so calm. It could
be this field of narcissus, lilac, the water milfoil,
the white petals of wild ginger. It could be
the blue irises, the honeysuckle and woodbine.

It could be the yellow flocks of parrots. Perhaps
it's the wind spreading seeds: tansy, sesame,
fennel. Perhaps it's this odd feeling I have that
someone today will fill my bowl with rice gruel.

A Dire Season

A star had appeared in the night sky,
it was long and pointed as an adder's tooth.
The moon rose putrescent, bloody. All our
elephants had turned viridian-eyed, wild.
Dozens of snakes hissed as though a fierce
wind blew. Many children fell ill,

tottered on legs like blown-up bladders.
All we could do was summon the Brahmins,
watch as they poured ghee over the altars
and burnt our cattle in sacrifice. After a week
we had little left to offer, though we still
dug fields, hauled water, turned the loam.

We all felt Kapilavatthu was done for,
that not one of those Brahmins had the verses
to save us. We drank bitter herbs,
flailed our skin with twigs we bought
from the broom makers, cut our arms
with shards from the potters' workshops.

We fingered crimson beads and performed
small dry ceremonies in the dirt. Before
that season finally turned, I'd often long
for Siddhattha, for the little tunes he could play
on his thin, twisted stems of grass.
Something about his notes, their fine weaving

through the dusk. When I listened, I thought
of our clay daub, mud brick and whitewashed
town as a grand place, one whose streets
you could walk down squaring your shoulders,
knowing that the gods supped at the flames
that burnt on our altars. I don't know

what Siddhattha heard in the notes.
Perhaps he foresaw the rise of the rivers,
border conflicts in the west, heard the screams
of our women and children, saw the smoke
and the fires, saw Kapilavatthu overrun
with Brahmins carrying slaughtered oxen

and antelope aloft from all our fire hearths –
all that blood and dung,
all the vulture feathers in their topknots.

Angulimala

Angulimala, thug and robber, who once wore
a necklace made from the knuckles of those he'd murdered,
has joined the Order. Angulimala is now shaven-headed
and yellow-robed! How did Buddha swing him over?

Ah, but perhaps it's a ruse. Angulimala would know
the monastery is free from the law, he may think
he can hide here. But if he has changed, if the Buddha
has made him meek as a calf, it's a great coup;

the townsfolk will be so thankful, they'll give us
more alms, put less in other mendicants' bowls. Then every
beggar will turn cloak, come over to us and the Order
will be bigger, all the better for me to finally

take hold of. So maybe I'll look after Angulimala,
stay by his side on his rounds, watch no-one tears his robes,
stones him, shatters his bowl... One day, I may even
give him a purse full of Siddhattha's knucklebones.

My Potential Conversation with Siddhattha

Cousin, if one day you see a gibbon and a chameleon mate,
if you see eels or other fishes of the night waters, the night tides,
crawl on the earth at midday, if you see an antelope
and a cobra switch ground, if you see a mole
and a mongoose battle for supremacy in the sycamores –
then you'll know your monks have begun throwing cowpats,

burning their doormats, demanding bigger bowls, better bedding,
a little luxury. You'll know each monk will be back-chatting
more than the monkeys and the grivets in the pomegranates.
If you hear a vulture in the town square bellow,
if you see an ox ride a dromedary, a flamingo kill a mountain lion,
an elephant prostrate itself before a locust or a dragonfly,

if you see a donkey whose semen is fire, sleep soundly
in a stable of jennies, a storehouse of barley,
you'll know the monks are belching, burping, chatting raucously
as they eat, having robbed several farmers and merchants
of rice and sweetmeats. You could be forgiven then,
cousin, for thinking the moon has turned to marrow fat,

that the Ganges flows backwards, that all certainties,
all polarities have been reversed or blistered away
by men whose hearts are the cinders and ash
of the most bitter, lixiviated wood. Not so, Siddhattha.
Just one man is enough to tip the tide and turn all things awry.
A tightness in his mind and heart, a perverse lust.

Return

Sometimes I like to imagine
what might happen if ever I returned to Kapilavatthu.
Perhaps all that day
there would be the smell
of rosemary, cumin and roasting goat.
The townsfolk
might string their bows and raise them high
over their heads and sing songs of good fortune
and plentiful harvests; they might slaughter
several oxen and then after much
laughter and cheering, they will decree
that in my honour
the streets shall be washed down with myrrh.
The merchants in Lumbini will be owed a fortune
for the wine,
even beyond what a year's fasting can provide,
but everyone will be happy,
falling drunk across the tables
and someone will play a sitar till dawn.

For several days afterwards
the whole of Kapilavatthu will smell sweet
with my return.
Everyone will forget the days they've struggled,
straggling across fields trying to salvage
what remains of their lives.

They'll forget the plundering neighbours,
the smoke of burning huts,
that Sakiya is a slave state to Kosala.

All they'll think about
will be how they dance in spangled red garments
on light-struck earth;
honey, spices and patriotic speeches
congealing in their mouths.
All they'll think about
will be that Devadatta has come back and about how
their lives, at last,
feel as precious as silk
pulled through a ring.

The View

Whenever I'd grow fed up with disputes between the farmers
and the money lenders, when I'd grow bored with Statecraft,
I'd walk up to the foothills of the Mahabharata Range.
There I'd forget about Kapilavatthu, forget how Sakiya
would always be a vassal state to Kosala. I'd forget about

the frontier conflicts in the west, that the newly federated
republics were squabbling. I'd watch the freshets
tumble into the almond groves and I'd smell the milk and fleece
from broad-horned sheep. I'd stare up towards the ice
peaks and watch the sunlight empty through the clouds

like pink-tinctured whey strained through veils of cheesecloth.
I'd watch stars, flakes of garnishing silver, cover the sky
as if it were a platter of festive sweets. Here, there's nothing
but the flat iron-red plains, clumps of earth in a marinade
of yesterday's rain, skies heavy and black as any

cast iron pot. When I grow irritable with myself,
even with my own shadow, there seems nowhere to go,
nowhere to look towards, only down at my face mirrored
in my alms bowl, or at ibises scavenging, or at the moon
worn as a bone protruding from a charnel mound.

Karma

I'm sick of your words Siddhattha, sick of your impeccable
gestures, of seeing how much the townsfolk love you;
how women swoon whenever they see you gather up
the folds of your robe with a lithe, muscular arm before
you cross the street to beg among their bamboo houses.

I'm sick of hearing your voice like oil running along
watered silk. I want your face, Siddhattha, to turn
as wan as the face of that Brahmin over there in the field,
stretching the throats of sheep and heifers for the blade –
and then suddenly realising, the last sacrifice he'll lay

on Agni's altar, is himself on the flaming funeral pyre.
I want to see your countenance, cousin, when I pull you
down from your bastion of equanimity; when I no longer
have the shyness of a gazelle – but the cunning of a crocodile,
the greed of a monkey, the invidiousness of a snake,

the skill of a merchant manipulating the scales always
to his advantage. I want to see your eyes, Siddhattha,
when I no longer care if my next birth is from the egg
of a louse, a worm, a flea spreading contagion; or from
the womb of a rodent, a bitch – even a shameless harridan.

Nightmare

Lately a rogue elephant has been entering
my dreams, thrusting me against rocks, trying to crush
me by rolling me with its tusks. Then the dream
mutates and the thick horrible stench of musth
sweetens to musk, and those tusks take on

the roundness of breasts, and the trunk becomes
a soft, swaying braid of hair. When I wake
I barely recall the stomping feet, the wildly
flailing tusks. I remember the light-dusted face
of a woman moving voluptuously towards me –

but then suddenly she flinches, pulls back,
refuses me touch. I'd rather remember
the crushing tusks, the suffocating musth
than the look on her face as she loses her lust. Such
a heavy pain to wake with, the pain of her rebuff.

At the Lake

Today I don't care about Sariputta or Magallana, darlings
of the dharma, in their huts perfecting postures, working their way
towards Nirvana, tight in the Buddha's inner cell.
I'm out loafing. I'm a lotus-eater and a lummox.
I'm as oafish as a blowfly at noon, sitting on my buttocks

as a slackening tide tickles my toes. Yesterday I swotted,
I was studious, I boned up on deceit, treachery, betrayal.
Until well into the dawn, my lamp burnt reasting oils.
Today I stooge about on the shank of an afternoon.
I sit with the ducks that flunk air school and we quack

at the egrets. I'm a sloucher, a sluggard. Today the lake
and the sun can perfect the shining hour. Tomorrow
I'll study again and brew. I'll work out how to sully
the Buddha's lily-white Order; how to get hordes of townsfolk
to drive the bickering bhikkhus right out of Rajagaha.

A Memory: Snake Charming, Kapilavatthu

It's hard to believe Siddhattha didn't connect my snakes'
sluing and slanting with my flute's rhythmic sway.
He'd pipe until he was out of breath, baffled because
he always reached perfect notes, perfect pitch.

I swore I wouldn't tell him it didn't matter
if he played melodic notes, discordant notes, or no notes
at all, that just by swinging his flute-tip in the air
his snakes would rise like fluent rope. I felt such delight

letting him believe his music was impotent, letting him
strain and blow and swell his cheeks to deliver ever more
hapless sounds. The day Yasodhara came to see us practise

it gave me such bliss to watch my snakes rise and sway
like the sensuous arms of court dancers, while Siddhattha's
remained a knotted bolus at the bottom of the basket.

Nalagiri

This mahout wants cattle, frankincense, gold –
'too much!' – but I can hear Nalagiri bellow in her stall.
When she stomps her feet, I sense the iron madness
in her eyes. The mahout grins, rubs his hands,
adds silver, brass and alabaster to his price.

This sharp-faced man thinks he has my measure.
He thinks the image of his beast wandering
Rajagaha's streets, juggling pieces of Siddhattha's
shattered skull across her wide, gut-garlanded tusks
will make me generous. I'll not let him know

one day I'll come again, how I'll be dreaming
of her hot-headed bellowing, of her run-amok,
blood-bespattered tusks. When I come back,
I'll bring figs, grapes, pomegranates, gold-vermillion
melons – the best, the sweetest – for this malfeasant beast.

The Hermit

Some days we tell each other things easier to trust,
but most days we talk blabber and a load of balderdash.
I tell him I was a cloth dyer from Benares and I stole
a bolt of silk from a trader, then I hid in a hollow tree

for safety. He tells me a similar tale, but the white ants
ate the silk and all the clothes off his back, so for months
he wandered naked. I tell him I once earned a living
divining people's futures from rat bites. He tells me

he lived in a large earthenware salt jar on a riverbank
outside Rajkote (he's very hunchbacked, so you *could*
believe it). I tell him about Nalagiri, the mad elephant,
about my plans for the Sangha and for the Buddha.

At this he giggles, winks a pawky eye, says, 'Devadatta,
you talk such trash!' as if he knows he can put this lot
down to my grandiloquent manner, my theatrical panache,
perhaps to my overconsumption of his Nepalese hash.

On the Road, after another Rains Retreat

There's moonlight over the grass this morning, silver
as the pelt of an old gibbon. Down in the valley a few huts
and buffalo grazing. I see women by the river carrying
basketfuls of cloth. Soon they will hang the dyed fabric
over bushes which will be as bright as trees in their

wet season blossoms. I look at the terraced rice fields,
at the dawn turning the eastern sky a pale guava,
at the moon full as an alms offering of barley and honey.
What could be more beautiful than this early sun
striking this city's gates, glinting off the bronze inlays?

I turn towards the plain where dust from the oxherd
caravans rises up. Perhaps sometime today, people
will say that Devadatta has left, taken the journey south.
Perhaps someone will slaughter a goat, pray for me
by the town pond. Where I'll be by dusk, I cannot say,

but I know there's a great sweep of air beyond, breezes
bringing the pungent but delicate smell of pepper
and timber. Perhaps one day I may wake with the honest
face of someone who has slept on hard ground, someone
who has tried to travel part of the way on his knees.

On My Way to Benares

Smoke over the stubbled field of the pumpkins,
hunting dogs eating the umbles of a deer. In the west
a spree of birds and an old man under the pull
of his cart dragging a load of rubble and wood.
I haul my donkey into a pomegranate's shade,

the animal jostles, snorts, stomps, tries to chomp
through its goat-hair reins. It drops its muzzle –
begins braying for barley, broomcorn, sassafras –
it's so cantankerous it refuses to budge.
I'm desperate to get to Benares for the madcap

frivolity of a festival, for the wine, sweetmeats
and stuffed breads. There's no fodder anywhere,
not one stalk of chaff...Ah, wait, there's a crippled
old hag lying on a millet palliasse. I'll drag
it out from under her. Feed that to the jackass.

Daybreak

I watch day break over the dew-tipped fields of hyacinth,
amaryllis, alyssum and then across the hillsides
of furze. But I can only look for a short time before
I think of the light glittering along Yasodhara's hair
whenever it fell from her shoulders. Here, the flurrying
insects and dry leaf sounds are *hers, hers* – and always

I'm the voyeur dreaming her myrrh-tipped fingers
are touching my lips, tousling my hair. What I wouldn't
suffer to sweep my gaze across her face; to ply a hand
through her hair lit by the first stirrings of dawn,
to feel those strands furl into my fingers. I sigh, look away.
I'm weary of trying to turn everything into a fantasy;

weary of trying to set down my load and staring into
the abyss. O, let the furze, the alyssum, the hyacinth,
purled in dawn's glow, seem humdrum, plain.
Let the yellow just pull across the hillside, the sun
stand above the mountain. Let me not see the amaryllis
turn into one more merciless, untouchable shade of bliss.

Rocks, Vultures Peak

This rock's much too heavy for me to dislodge,
but I'll grab a tree limb and administer some torque.
I won't stir a pebble until he comes round the bend.
Ah, he's here now – I push – but the rock's fallen
far short. Did I move too soon? I didn't think he'd spend

so much time with the view, watching the birds,
watching the river pour through the valley.
He's barely injured. A cut on his toe. I sent down
granite, hornblende: large chunks, surely one, sharp
as a tomahawk, would've cracked open his skull?

Ah, one day Siddhattha, I'll pick the right spot,
I'll pick the right rock and I won't baulk the timing.
I know how the story will go: 'Slipping schist kills
local altruist.' 'Leader of cult, brained by basalt.'
'Religious moderate, crushed by conglomerate.'

My Discourse on Counting

Seven grains of very fine dust make a mote
you can see in a sunbeam. Seven motes make
a pollen grain. Four pollen grains make
a poppy seed, or the egg of a louse. Three sighs

make a yawn. Half a sigh makes the hoot
of an owl. Nine hoots of an owl make twenty
field mice squeal like one hairy boar
which makes forty flies buzz and seven rats

scurry into the pen and nibble into a firkin
of barleycorn. One barleycorn makes three weevils.
Three weevils make seventy-five harvest mites.
Ten wood ticks and a mealworm make a horsefly

that in a single hour can sting the rumps
of four mares, eight foals, seven geldings, two
bucking steeds, five mules and one cow pony.
When five cool winds meet nine hot winds,

the sky loses a pennyweight of its density.
Two water drops make a gecko's egg. Ten
gecko's eggs resemble the guano of the red-footed
turkey buzzard. One thousand turkey buzzards

contain uncountable lice. In the ten directions,
all winds are the one wind of the south.
In the north-east, all sounds are the thunder
of rocks falling down Vultures Peak. Seven falling

boulders make a cry in the land of Magadha,
wailing and keening in the state of Sakiya.
Three women wailing make a grave. One grave
can reincarnate into any number of graves.

Four Noble Truths make the ever-increasing
Sangha where one day my name will be written
into infinity and Siddhattha's will become a nullity,
a zero – his name never to be written anywhere,

not even on a stone with a piece of moon for chalk,
not even on a poppy seed, a barleycorn, the egg
of a louse, not on a weevil, a field mouse, a mote
in a sunbeam – not even on a grain of very fine dust.

Thinking of Kapilavatthu

Sometimes I wonder why I wobbled far into the distance
like an unhitched cart to bunker down to this life of alms,
slim pickings, lost hope. I cry for the blue and lilac
ring of hills and the shaded small valleys where I'd roam
as a child. Often I wake at night in a panic, thinking
Kapilavatthu has been invaded by sourly grimacing strangers
and their fiercely trained dogs. Do the other monks

ever grow homesick, or can they forget their agonies
of memory, the thicknesses of loss and just keep unerringly
returning to the present? Perhaps it's time to journey
home to see if dusty children still roam in the streets,
if mothers cradle infants in the shadows of their doorways;
if women still slap clothes onto stones to the accompaniment
of their delicate glass bangles. I long for the bazaars

and shaded streets, the town square full of the fragrant
scents of cedar and pine, the ornaments of the dancing girls
tinkling as they step. Tonight, all I can hear are ox toads
mooing as fatuously as an assembly of chanting monks,
the wind's drawn-out *alas* through top branches of a sassafras,
rats and cobras bearing through the grass, and rain pouring
down my hut, one more long and boring Discourse.

Figurines

Traders would come to Kapilavatthu bringing exotic wares:
marine shells, brass mirrors, copper soft as the meat of dates.
Many brought figurines: tigers, antelopes, goats, tiny carnelian
figures with human faces and the tails of hooded snakes.

I'd buy silver unicorns, ones with wide eyes, flaring nostrils
and tufted tails. Other boys bought humped bulls, or goats
that had twisted horns spreading to each side of their heads.
We'd play strategy games, argue, capture each other's pieces.

Siddhattha never joined in. He'd buy conch shells and spend
his time slowly chipping away at the apexes turning them
into sweet-toned trumpets. We laughed at him, sitting
at a distance, playing his notes. How each of us burned –

trying to make their animal the essence of a team's ploy,
a fortress's defence. We'd switch allegiances, make unholy
alliances between the rams, lions and goats; or take a risk
and try to win with a wax-carved donkey, or with the ewe

with a missing face. Always our games ended in fights:
smashed figurines, torn clothes, black eyes, bloody mouths
and noses. Ah, it's not the fights I can't bear remembering –
but Siddhattha sitting there, blowing his insouciant notes.

Dreaming of Yasodhara in the Rain

This rain's too heavy for me
to descend into sleep, so I conjure her again in the shadows
above my head. Already she's removed the lid from an alabaster jar
and has rubbed jasmine oil into her scalp, drawn saffron
across her forehead, lamp-black around her eyes.

Soon she'll step towards me
among the swollen blossoms of the night flowers, set honey cakes
upon the table and fan my brow with a mango branch. Again I hear
the rain, it could be gushing towards me through the sala trees,
the sycamores, the bamboo; washing away the clay huts,

the leafy burrows of the poor.
But let the fonts overflow, the banks break, because now we are
lying across the damson cushions of her sissoo wood seat;
with full-throated want she pours the bedlam drink. I can hear
the ox toads mooing. I can hear water spilling from the channels,

and I'm straining to tell if this hissing
is more of the frictional washing of the water through the leaves
outside, or the sound of vipers seeking refuge in my hut.
But then I see her toe rings sparkle. I smell the honeyed perfume
of her skin. I let her arms swaddle my cool weight in.

Kapilavatthu: Zoo

As boys, we were too young
for dancers or courtesans, so Siddhattha's father built us
a zoo. One day, bored, I crawled into a cage with the gibbons.
They paid me no mind, so I yelled, beat a stick

across the bars until they threw
urine-sodden leaves, rotting fruit and piles of dung at me.
When I was found I was scrubbed with lye, pummelled
with pumice stone; my hair was fettled over and over

with a hackle comb. I was thrown
head-first into a lotus pond. I can still remember my cries,
how all the other boys mocked and jeered. Only Siddhattha
tried to turn my sobs into giggles by tickling me with flicks

from his yak-hair flywhisk.
I thought of it this morning staring at the pond as a breeze
brought the cry of a gibbon from the forest, when a few leaves
blowing from the sala trees touched me so very tenderly.

Penance

Some nights, when all I do is scheme
to give Siddhattha schism, infighting, dissonance;
when I think of what a pleasure it will be
to give him 'dissentry' – then I plan some days
of penance: to lie among wood ticks, crickets,
the breaching heads of worms and leeches;
to let the gall borers gnaw my toes;
to offer the soft flanges around the tops
of my ears to the water fleas and wasps.
I'll let mosquitoes gather and fly off potbellied
with my blood. I won't apply saliva
or mud, use any unguents, no paste of cloves
and honey. Though the moon will mock me
like a pointed instrument, like a round
and cooling poultice, I won't give comfort
to any part of my body, but cover myself
with nettles, itch weed, with crow and turkey feathers,
with henhouse refuse so that mites, too,
can leave me scaled and scabbed.
I won't climb away from my skin
even if worms burrow, or web-spinning flies
hang threads in my beard and make slime.
Though my fingernails will have grown so long,
I'll not scratch a single bite, or strike any insect
down, but I'll palp them like antennae.

I'll lie on the forest floor among the burrows
of roaches and long-horned stag beetles,
and the sound closest to my ears will be the sound
of army ants devouring everything to pieces.

Notes

Throughout the sequence I have mostly used the Pāli spellings in preference to Sanskrit. I am also following the Theravada (Pāli) tradition's dating. The actual dates of all of these events are still being debated by scholars. Some of the references to plants and trees are not always geographically or historically accurate. Some names I have used for poetic effect.

Wanting Yasodhara: Yasodhara was the wife of Siddhattha. They married in approximately 547 BCE.

To Ananda: Ananda was Devadatta's brother and also a cousin to Siddhattha. He became a favourite disciple of the Buddha and constant attendant for the last twenty-five years of the Buddha's life. I have invented the name Raghaya Pond.

Back in the Monastery, Sarnath: The goddesses named in this poem are Hindu goddesses and are later deities than those which existed during Devadatta's time.

Tailspin: Dukkha is critical to an understanding of the Four Noble Truths. The Buddha taught that there are three main types of dukkha, translated broadly as suffering or dissatisfaction:

1. suffering or pain – physical, emotional or mental;
2. impermanence or change;
3. the fact that all phenomena are dependent and conditional.

The turning of the wheel of law refers to the preaching of the Buddha. The Buddha 'turned the wheel' of his teachings in order to subdue people's delusions and desires.

The Buddha at Uruvela: The names mentioned in this poem occurred previously in my poem, 'The Buddha Cycle' published in *Accidental Grace*.

In Rajagaha: Sariputta and Moggallana were two friends who became disciples of the Buddha in the Kingdom of Magadha. Sariputta has been praised for his analytical and philosophical intelligence. Moggallana was an especially gifted meditator. Both became the Buddha's chief disciples. The doctrine of the Four Noble Truths has the following components:

1. all existence is suffering;
2. suffering is caused by selfish craving;
3. selfish craving can be destroyed;
4. it can be destroyed by following the Eightfold Path.

The Eightfold Path consists of: 1. right view;
2. right resolve; 3. right speech; 4. right action;
5. right livelihood; 6. right effort; 7. right mindfulness;
8. right concentration.

The musical instrument, the sitar, is an instrument from a later period. I have used it for poetic effect.

Vultures Peak: Vultures Peak was situated on the southern slope of Mount Chatha, in Magadha. It had a fine view of the valley and was a favourite spot of the Buddha's. The phrase 'sinking madder sun' has been borrowed from John Ennis's poem, 'A Drink of Spring', published in *An Anthology of Modern Irish Poetry,* edited by Wes Davis, The Belknap Press of Harvard University Press, 2010.

Rules: Some of the details used in this poem are taken from T. Griffith Foulk's essay, 'Daily Life in the Assembly' published in *Buddhism in Practice,* edited by Donald

S. Lopez, Jr., Princeton University Press, 1995. The details in the poem actually apply to later Buddhist assemblies.

New Day: Rice gruel is a food made by boiling rice in milk with beans and butter. It was considered at the time to be a great delicacy.

Angulimala: Angulimala was the name of a robber and murderer. The name means 'Finger-necklace' because he made himself a necklace from the knuckles of people he had murdered. He was a member of a large criminal gang. In 508 BCE he was admitted by the Buddha into the Order of monks.

At the Lake: Nirvana is synonymous with the concept of liberation, which refers to release from a state of suffering after an often lengthy period of committed spiritual practice. In this state the mind has ended its identity with material phenomena and experiences a great sense of peace and a unique form of awareness. Bhikkhu is the Pāli word for disciple or mendicant, someone who had completed their period of training in the ascetic life and was respected by the population at large for that reason.

Nalagiri: Nalagiri was the name of the elephant that Devadatta bribed certain mahouts to let loose on the Buddha. This was also one of the ways Devadatta endeavoured to murder the Buddha. The elephant was purportedly male, though I have made it female.

The Hermit: The phrase 'Nepalese hash' is anachronistic. I have used it for poetic effect.

Rocks, Vultures Peak: Another of the ways in which Devadatta attempted to murder the Buddha was to drop a boulder on him as he passed under a cliff.

My Discourse on Counting: This poem was inspired by a passage in Robert Kaplan's book, *The Nothing That Is,* Penguin, 1995, p38–39: 'seven of the finest atoms make a grain of very fine dust, seven of which make a little grain of dust. Seven such grains make a mote you can see in a sunbeam, seven of these a rabbit's grain, seven rabbit's grains a ram's grain, seven ram's grains an ox's grain, seven ox's grains – a poppy seed!'

This project has been assisted by the Commonwealth Government through the Australia Council, its arts funding and advisory body.